ISBN 978-0-656-02457-5
PIBN 10289271

A GUIDE

OR

HAND-BOOK

FOR

Mount Hope Cemetery,

WITH

PHOTO-ENGRAVINGS AND DIAGRAM.

BY

EDWARD ANGEVINE

ROCHESTER, N. Y.

ROCHESTER, N.Y.:
DEMOCRAT AND CHRONICLE BOOK AND JOB PRINT.
1885.

DEDICATION.

This Guide or Hand-Book is· respectfully dedicated to NEWELL A. STONE, FREDERICK COOK; JOHN W. MARTIN, present Commissioners of Mount Hope; GEORGE T. STILLSON, the Superintendent, GEORGE G. COOPER, and JAMES H. KELLY, who served for many years as Commissioners with unwearying interest in the beautiful 'City of the Dead," and to the lot owners.

PREFACE.

The want of a Guide `or Hand-Book for Mount Hope Cemetery has long been felt by lot owners and the strangers who visit the place. To supply this want, the compilation and publication of this volume was undertaken. It should be welcomed by every one who has a dear relative or friend buried there. and by the thousands of visitors who seek the ground to admire all that is grand and beautiful in nature and the works of art, memorials of love and reverence to adorn the last resting place of those who are peacefully sleeping, awaiting the resurrection and glorious immortality.

It cannot be expected that every one of the thousands of lots, avenues, paths, etc., can be mentioned in a work of this character. If it assists the reader in a general way in finding the most attractive objects and locations, it will accomplish what was designed by the author. A day's ramble through the Cemetery by one not thoroughly acquainted with the formation of the grounds, the main avenues and sections, would prove unsatisfactory. With the Guide n hand

and an occasional glance at the diagram, an
intelligent tour can be made in two or three
hours.   A drive can be made in less time and
the principal objects viewed without leaving
the carriage.   There are nearly twelve thousand
lots in the Cemetery, and it will be seen that it is
an impossibility to mention more than a respect-
able and representative fraction of them.   Many
very pretty lots, tombstones and monuments
have nothing on them indicating the name of
the owner or the person buried. "Father,"
" Mother," " Sister," " Brother," "Baby," " Pet,"
etc., convey no information to the simple tourist,
while to visiting relative or friend they impart a
world of meaning and awaken tender memories.

Every citizen of Rochester has an interest in
Mount Hope.

> " There is no flock, however watched and tended,
>   But one dead lamb is there !
> There is no fireside, howsoe'er defended,
>   But has one vacant chair."

HISTORICAL SKETCH.

Soon after the incorporation of the City of Rochester, the matter of locating a new Cemetery was agitated. Several localities were suggested. The lamented William A. Reynolds was in favor of selecting the western banks of Irondequoit Bay.

On the 24th of August, 1836, in the Common Council, Alderman David Scoville offered a resolution that a committee be appointed to inquire into the expediency of purchasing Silas Andrus' lot on the east side of the river " or any other lot in the city," for a burial ground and report at a future meeting of the Board. The first purchase was made of Silas Andrus, of Hartford, Conn., Jan. 2, 1837, being $53\frac{86}{100}$ acres for which the then large sum of $100 an acre was paid. The earliest sale on record of this land as a distinct tract was April 30, 1817, when Elijah Northrup sold it to Eli Stillson, grandfather of the present Superintendent of Mount Hope, for $367. Mr. Stillson sold it to John Mastick, July 12, 1821, for $262, who sold it to Silas Andrus, January 1, 1822, for $287, and Mr.

Andrus fifteen years later sold it to the City of Rochester for $5,386. Being just prior to the panic of 1837, values were greatly inflated. Including this land the different purchases to the present day have been as follows :

When bought.	Acres.	Cost.	Owner.
1837—Jan. 2...	53.86	$5,386.00	Silas Andrus.
1837—Dec. 9...	1.21	nom.	
1839—Aug. 22.	9.39	1,875.00	Wm. Hamilton.
1841—April 15.	9.02	902.00	D. Stanley.
1861—July 29..4.2157		3,000.00	Moses Hall.
1864—June 15..	5.33	1,440 90	Caleb Pierce.
1864—June 21..	7.82	1,947.79	Caleb Pierce.
1865—Jan. 25..	23.66	3,000.00	Eleazer Conkey.
1865—May 1...	52.17	20,864.00	A. F. & G. P. Wolcott.
1865—Nov. 3..	32.74	9,096.00	B. F. & Maria Hall.
1872—April 3..	19	16,200.00	Heirs Hamilton estate.
	200.00	$63,711.69	

DEDICATION OF MT. HOPE.

The Cemetery was dedicated October 3, 1838, three months subsequent to the first interment. The dedicatory address was delivered by Rev. Pharcellus Church, pastor of the First Baptist Church of Rochester. The following extract is taken from his address :

> The rural and picturesque scenery with which we are surrounded, strikingly harmonizes with the object which has called us together. We have come to consecrate a home for the dead in which they may rest secure from the encroachments of industry and avarice till the last trumpet calls them to judgment. Among these sequestered shades the living tenants of a bustling city will soon find repose.

Forty-seven years have fled since these words were uttered by the venerable preacher. Nearly forty-five thousand of our dead now sleep in the consecrated grounds, more, far more, than the population of the " bustling city " at the time of the dedication. Another half century and Mount Hope's inhabitants will exceed the present population of Rochester. With a thousand interments annually, it is not surprising that the interest of the living in caring for and beautify-

ing the grounds grows apace. There are many
still living who heard the dedicatory address,
but the great majority have joined the "in-
numerable throng" before "The Great White
Throne."

The old entrance, Superintendent's office,
waiting-rooms, etc., built in 1859, at a cost of a
trifle over $10,000, were removed 1874, and the
present entrance and structure erected at a cost
of $17,000. James H. Kelly, Newell A. Stone
and William S. Smith were then commissioners.
In 1860 the present chapel and receiving vault
were built at cost of $10,000. The structure has
a pleasing exterior, but a gloomy, unpleasant
interior, and is not of sufficient size. Of late
years much attention has been given by the lot
owners, who number over 10,000, to the improve-
ment of the grounds. Many costly and beautiful monuments and vaults have been erected,
creditable to the living and enduring memorials
to the dead.

The valley to the left of the entrance and in
front of the chapel was an unsightly swamp,
unsuitable for burial purposes. The late Geo.
D. Stillson, who, more than any other man made
Mount Hope the beautiful place it is, construct-
ed a tunnel through it, draining the water into
the Genesee river. The tunnel runs directly
under the Chapel and Receiving Vault. It is a

grand monument to his engineering skill. He rests from his labors near by, and many a tribute is paid to his memory by those who pass his tomb. Mount Hope was his idol and loving care. It is fitting that he sleeps amid its beauties. The lands thus reclaimed and utilized by him, now form one of the handsomest localities in the Cemetery. [See engraving].

PERPETUAL REPAIR CONTRACT.

The adoption of an ordinance by the City of Rochester, in 1872, provides for the perpetual repair and care of lots and graves, from the interest of a certain sum deposited for that purpose. The lot owner, in availing him or herself of this privilege is assured of the fulfillment of the obligation on the part of the City, through the Commissioners and Superintendent of the Cemetery, aside from the satisfaction of contributing to the general appearance of the ground. The following are the leading provisions of the ordinance :

SEC. 1. Any person may pay to the Treasurer of Mt. Hope Cemetery, a sum of money not less than ten or more than one thousand dollars, for the purpose of keeping in order any lot or parcel of land in such Cemetery, and thereafter the interest obtained on such sum, shall, from time to time, as occasion may require, be expended on such lot or parcel of land by or under the direction of the Commissioners of said Cemetery.

SEC. 2. The Treasurer of Mt. Hope Cemetery shall immediately deposit such sums of money in such Savings Bank or banks as the Commissioners of said Cemetery shall direct, which moneys shall be kept in special deposit on interest apart from all other moneys belonging to Mt. Hope Cemetery.

SEC. 7. In no event shall the City ever be liable to repay the principal paid under this ordinance, but shall be liable for the faithful discharge of its provisions.

Many persons who invested in the perpetual repair fund have since died, leaving no relative or friend to look after their lots or graves. Yet they are cared for and the interest on investment expended on them and will continue to be. The other rules and regulations of the Cemetery are temporary, to be changed as expediency requires, but the above contract is unalterable. The neat appearance of the Dr. Carver lot is a notable illustration of the working of the ordinance.

MOUNT HOPE.

Nature designed Mount Hope for the last resting place of those who "pass beyond the vale." The ridges, the hills, the valleys and dells, the sloping banks and terraced walks and paths, the lawns, the trees whose trunks are entwined with brilliantly tinted woodbine, the willows with their arching branches, the stately oak and chestnut, among whose limbs the pretty squirrel disports, suggests that here the "weary are at rest."

Here the great mother guards her holy trust,
Spreads her green mantle o'er the sleeping dust ;
Here glows the sunshine, here the branches wave,
And birds yield song, flowers' fragrance round the graves.
Here oft to hold communion do we stray,
Here droops our mourning memory when away,
And e'er when years have passed our homeward feet,
Seek first with eager haste this spot to greet,
And the fond hope lives ever in our breast,
When death too claims us, here our dust shall rest.

[*A. B. Street.*]

The entrance building for offices and waiting rooms, is of cut stone and is a creditable structure. The gate-ways add to its appearance. Inside the gate the visitor enters upon a wide, smooth, graveled roadway. Passing a handsome drinking fountain on the right, the ground rises gradually to Indian Trail Avenue, with a carriage road and flag walk. The road on the left gently slopes into the valley, to the doors of the Chapel

and continues on to Indian Trail Avenue, near
Sylvan Waters; it is called Ravine Avenue.
Just beyond the point of bifurcation of these
avenues, is a large circular lawn ; in the center
a flower mound thirty feet in diameter, and in
the center of that, an elegant fountain which
throws hundreds of sparkling jets of water high
into the air. Between the Chapel and the carriage road on the right before mentioned, is the
fine vault of the late Gen. Jacob Gould and the
granite mausoleum of Charles Rau. The view
in this valley is faithfully reproduced in the
engraving. The two largest monuments seen
on the second lawn are those of John E. Morey,
Sr., and of the late Dr. John B. Elwood. The
Morey monument is one of the best proportion-
ed in Mount Hope, and is very conspicuous
from many points of view ; the bases and shaft
are of granite ; a marble figure representing
" Faith," surmounts the shaft ; it is an exceed-
ingly fine piece of sculpture, the work of an
eminent Italian sculptor, and is much admired.
South-westerly and on the west side of Ravine
Avenue in Section F. is the family vault of the
late Lewis H. Morgan. It is of red sand stone
and the interior is catacombed. Lewis H. Morgan
was one of the most distinguished ethnological
and archaeological scholars and authors of his
time. At his death, 1881, he was President of the

American Association for the advancement of science.

Before ascending to Indian Trail Avenue, for the purpose of economizing time and labor, we turn to the right and enter upon Section D. one, of the nicest sections in the Cemetery. The whole of it is in full view from the public highway Mount Hope Avenue. The ground slopes gradually from the ridge toward the Avenue. There are many nice monuments and lots on this section, notably those of Lewis Brooks, Richards and Weaver, James Stewart, Junius Judson, Azariah Boody, Wm. Maguire, Caroline M. Thompson, Royal C. Knapp, C. Priem, M. Filon. A pretty headstone bearing engraved Masonic emblems, marks the grave of the late George W. Aldridge. In this section are the lots of Geo. A. Stone, James Vick, Jr., (dark granite headstone), Geo. and Conrad Herzberger, Henry Norden, Calvin Townsend, John G. Mutchler, Col. E. E. Sill, George W. Sill, F. Goetzman, Don Alonzo Watson, Thomas Leighton, H. Austin Brewster, Philander Cunningham, Romanta Hart, C. F. Wolters, Wm. Graebe, Henry L. Becker, Philip Bender, B. L. Sheldon, E. P. Shaffer. H. T. King, E. E. Bausch, S. J. Arnold, F. Fritzsche, F. Roth, John Hartel, Henry Walzer, Norman Day, (an elegant monument). We here cross the northern extension of

Indian Trail Avenue, and are upon Sec. C. which extends to the limits of the Cemetery on the west and north. The Genesee river runs at the foot of the bluff. A wedge shaped piece of land which runs south on the east side of Indian Trail Avenue, to a point in rear of the Chapel, in included in Sec. C. Linden Ave. is the main avenue running north and south, and Maple Ave. east and west in Sec. C. This ground is laid out in handsome and spacious lots, and there are many elegant and costly monuments. In the center is a large flower mound and a beautiful fountain. Among conspicuous monuments and lots are those of Casper Eckhardt, George W. Archer, John Vicinus, O. W. Moore, James Campbell, A. J. Hatch, Elon Huntington, Wm. N. Sage, E. S. Hayward, Simon L. Brewster, Levi S. Fulton, R. A. Sibley, Wright and David Todd, David Upton, Judge James L. Angle and J. A. Stull. The Fulton monument, though not large, is very handsome. This and the Eckhardt monument is of Richmond granite, the shafts surmounted with figures. Both came from the works of H. S. Hebard. Geo. H. Thompson's lot is close to the edge of the bluff. Here rests the late noble man whose name is inscribed on the fine granite monument. He was for a number of years a commissioner of Mount Hope, and took great pride in beautifying and making it one of the loveliest Cemeteries in the country. He strongly urged the author of this work to engage in the labor of its preparation and publication. He was greatly beloved and respected in the City of Rochester, where he was born and where he died. His was an active life of usefulness to himself and others. Peace to his ashes. In this immediate vicinity are the lots of Newell A. Stone and Frederick Cook, Commissioners of Mt. Hope, Jacob Gerling and A. G. Yates. A granite sarcophagus graces the Yates lot. The cap has polished edges and upon it is an ornamental cross. It was put up by Trott & Weigand. F. Ziegler, R. Sauerteig, A. Spahn, and other prominent Germans of Rochester have in Sec. C. near the fountain, almost directly in the rear of the Superintendent's dwelling house a cluster of fine lots. The Sauerteig monument is a very pretty one.

In this section are also the lots of Philip Will, H. Bartholomay, Col. S. S. Eddy, D. L. Johnston, Philip Block, F. Schlegel, H. S. Briggs, Geo. H. Newell, Kate Lee Ashley, (here is buried the lamented Col. A. T. Lee), H. T. Huntington, Calvin, Nathan, Elon and Geo. Huntington, Martin Joiner, Benjamin McFarlin, Wm. Knight, Calvin Huson, Chas. F. Smith, Dr. T. A. Proctor, John Bower, Chas. W. Briggs,

Wm. H. Bosworth, M. J. Monroe, Mrs. Anna G. Christensen, (lately deceased), F. Ruckdeschel.

On the left, ascending by stone steps to the surface of a terraced bluff, we are on a plateau where are many very handsome lots. This is Sec. A. We note the lots of H. H. Warner, S. V. McDowell, Frank W. Embry, and the late Dr. D. M. Shipman. There is a fine monument on the latter. Especially worthy of study are the head stones on the lot of Mr. McDowell. They are of statuary marble and have artistically carved flowers and vines on the panels. They were made by Trott & Weigand. Close by was lately laid to rest John W. Canfield, who was one of Rochester's most prominent young business men. His death was generally lamented. A little south of this Wm. B. Burke has a fine lot. Mr. Warner's lot ere long will be supplied with a monument creditable to the cultivated taste and liberality of that gentleman. Before leaving this spot notice what a beautiful view of the river and city can be obtained. Walking easterly and descending to Linden Avenue, near its junction with Maple Avenue, we re-enter Sec. C. We here confront the colossal monument of the late Isaac Butts. He who was recently so prominent in the political, social and business circles of the country, sleeps here, and beside him his beloved wife Mary, who died blessed by thousands for a multitude of generous deeds of charity. Just on the right a Lockport limestone monument denotes the burial place of Daniel Anthony, who had a world wide reputation as one of the original abolitionists, the friend of the oppressed in all lands. The monument was erected by his son, the Hon. D. R. Anthony, of Kansas. It bears on its face the words "Humanity," "Liberty," "Equality," "Justice." He ended his labors here Nov. 25th, 1862. His mantle fell on the shoulders of his talented and philanthropic daughter, Susan B. Anthony, and all the world admires how worthily she has borne it. Here also are the lots of D. C. Ellis, J. W. McKindley, Gerry S. Copeland, and the lamented John W. McElhenney. The monument on the lot of Geo. D. Waite is a fine one. In this vicinity, in Sec. A. a tombstone marks the spot where lies the dust of William Carter, who was the first person buried in the Cemetery. An inscription records the event. Giles Carter, a son of the deceased, is still living in Rochester. His father's interment occurred Aug. 18, 1838. Quite near to Mr. Carter's is the tomb of good old Prof. Dewey of High School fame, and whose memory is cherished by the "Old School Boys" of Rochester. He died in 1867, aged 84. He was a venerated instructor. Another pioneer, Josiah Bissell, of stage coach fame, and close by Zebulon and Martha, the father and mother of Henry S. Hebard, sleep peacefully. Andrew Semple and wife, father and mother of Andrew M. Semple, have here awaited for many years the summons of the putting on of immortality.

We have faced to the south on Sec. C. and are back of the Chapel. Here are the stately monuments and fine lots of John Robb and Samuel Wilder. On the right is the elevated lot of A. J. Johnson. The front wall is faced with red sandstone, with steps of the same material leading to the surface. Here reposes Johnson I. Robbins,. for years a prominent resident of Rochester. Directly over the chapel is buried Geo. B. Harris, who for years was a prominent fireman and public officer. No one knew better the history of Rochester and its old and leading citizens than he did. The late Henry Wray is buried near the Johnson lot. We note here also the lot of D. M. Dewey, located in the early days of the Cemetery.

Turning half around to the right, via Glen Ave., we descend into the finest valley in the Cemetery. Secs. U and R. are on our left. On the western slope of the hill is located the Reynolds lot, one of the handsomest in Mount Hope. The heavy granite coping is in pleasing contrast with the green sward and its paths of white pebbles. The family monument, of granite, is an elegant one. The tablets bear the inscriptions, "Abelard Reynolds, born 1785; died 1878." "William A. Reynolds, born 1810; died 1872." Here also sleeps the sleep of the blessed, Mary Hart, the beloved wife of Mortimer F. Reynolds. She departed this life in 1879. The relict of the lamented Abelard Reynolds reached her hundredth year Sept. 22d, 1884. It will be but a little while before she is laid beside her late husband and son. It needs no stately pile of marble or granite to commemorate the virtues and lives of Abelard and William A. Reynolds. One has only to cast his eye northward over the bustling City of Rochester to see their enduring memorial.

The lots of Dr. Thos. Arner, Ira Cook, (Sec. W.) and A. S. Mann, (Sec. R.) are on this slope. Each has a costly monument. The shaft of Mr. Mann's supports a large marble figure representing "Faith." In the east bank of Sec. R. facing Glen Ave., is the fine vault of Mrs. Mary Fitch. Near the Reynolds lot, lately there was given to mother earth the mortality of the wife of Policeman George Long. A brown stone monument just beyond marks the tomb of the late Dr. L. Kuichling, father of Emil Kuichling.

Ascending a flight of steps on our way to the summit, or Rochester Hill, a small and pretty monument marks the spot where sleeps Dr.

John Fonda Whitbeck, who died Dec. 8, 1880, an event which carried poignant sorrow into hundreds of households where he had been the loved and revered physician for thirty years. Society generally mourned his loss, and the City of Rochester lost one of its most eminent professional men, one who in his ministrations to the sick knew not the distinctions of wealth and poverty. His kindness and aid to the younger members of the profession, made him their idol. His services at the City Hospital will ever be gratefully remembered. He had served as President of the Monroe County Medical Society, City Medical Society, and was a member of the State and National societies. All of these bodies took appropriate action on his death, Dr. Chas. Buckley and others paying eloquent tributes to his memory. As prelate of Cyrene Commandery he was cotemporaneous with Abelard Reynolds of Monroe Commandery, and both now sleep in Mount Hope, very near each other, while a little further up the hill his friend and beloved brother in the profession, Dr. H. F. Montgomery is at rest. He was born at Claverack, Columbia Co., Sept. 27, 1812. His wife Mrs. L. E. Whitbeck, Dr. John W. Whitbeck and Mrs. C. R. Parsons survive him.

Just northwest of this spot is the pretty plat of Judge John S. Morgan.

Originally there was a large knoll on the north side of this prominence, and it was known as "Revolutionary Hill," not "Patriot Hill," and here in 1841, the bones of Lieut. Boyd and his com patriots in Sullivan's army were interred with great pomp and ceremony. It was intended also as the burial - place of revolutionary soldiers. The bones of Lieut. Boyd were placed in a wooden urn, which crumbled from exposure to the weather, and they became scattered. Some of them were secured by persons now residing in Rochester and are kept by them as relics. There were those who proclaimed that the bones were not those of Lieut Boyd, but Mr. George H. Harris, the most eminent authority in Western New York on the subject, produces incontrovertible proof that they were. The knoll was cut down in 1864 by Chauncey Parsons, who was the Superintendent, obliterating the historic spot.

> Gather him to his grave again,
>   And solemnly and softly lay,
> Beneath the verdure of the plain,
>   The Warrior's scattered bones away.

By the removal of the knoll the slope was made to form an ellipses forty feet in diameter.

The summit of this section is called Rochester Hill. The pedestal of the monument of Robert Hunter supports a cross, and a broken column of granite on the same lot indicates the grave of Ex-Mayor A. Carter Wilder. All the members of the Rochester, Montgomery, Child, Hart and Hunter families who have departed this life are buried here, including Col. Nathaniel Rochester who died in 1831, and after whom the City of Rochester was named ; and Jonathan Child who was the first Mayor of the City, in 1834. Brevet-Major Charles S. Montgomery, who commanded the 5th N. Y., S. V. Regt., and who was killed in action before Petersburg, Va., Feb. 6, 1865, sleeps here.

> Freedom hollows with her tread,
> The silent cities of the dead,
> And beautiful in death are they
> Who proudly fall in her array.

Close by is the tomb of Enos Stone, the first settler in Rochester, and the graves of others noted as the early pioneers of the Flower City.

Here also awaits the last trumpet call, Harvey F. Montgomery, who was one of the most prominent physicians of Rochester. His memory will always be cherished. Glen Avenue separates sections N. and R.

Having noted so many of the prominent objects on this section, the tourist has two routes open to him, first by crossing directly to Indian Trail Avenue, second, by returning to the entrance point. The latter route is the one we will take,

first remarking that Section W. is west or toward the river. The most prominent object there is the tomb and monument of Judge Wm. Buell, who left this sphere many years ago. Down in a dell on this section are interred most of the bodies removed from the old Buffalo and Monroe Streets burying grounds. The graves do not present the appearance of having much care. This would be a good place to compare the workings of the present perpetual contract system.

As we start for the Indian Trail Avenue, section B. is on our left or north. The family lot of George C. Buell is here nicely located. It is enclosed by a free stone fence, and graced by a fine monument. A tomb stone a little to the right bears this inscription: " Wickins Killick, his wife and five children who died within the space of ten days in September, 1854, of cholera. Finely situated is the family lot of the late Colon G. Wilson and Henry C. Daniels. Here only a few weeks ago were deposited the remains of the beloved wife of the latter. Her love of Mt. Hope when living was a passion.

We are again on Indian Trail Avenue facing south. Section U. is in the valley on our right, and Section F. after passing the south line of Section C. on our left. In Sections U. and R. are the tombs of John T. Lacey, Joseph Depoe and Aaron Lovecraft. The sloping bank is dotted with graves, and presents a handsome appearance. We pass on our left the lots and monuments of Raphael Beach, Ezra Jones, Seth C. Jones and Edward Roggen. On the crest of the ridge, Section F. near the vault of Lewis H. Morgan, is the lot, surrounded with a fine stone coping, of John Weiss, on which much money and care has been expended. A large grass plat defined by Hope and Indian Trail Avenues, was formerly the Firemen's lot. Section K. is on the south side of Hope Avenue, and in conformation is like unto the sole of a man's foot. Almost the first grave seen is that of Porter P. Pierce, who was murdered ·in Rochester in 1848, an incident remembered with great distinctness by the elderly residents of the City. On the old Firemen's lot are the burial places of G. Tallinger, Alfred Bell, Roswell Hart, and Dr. Jonas Jones, all having tasty and elegant monuments, of monolith, obelisk and sarcophagus styles. On the rounding corner of Hope and Ravine Avenues, is where George D. Stillson awaiteth the time when this mortality shall put on immortality. It is also the family lot of George T. Stillson. On the east side of Ravine Avenue, on Section L. is the grave and monument of Elias P.ond, and near the Stillson lot is the burial lot of George and Thomas Raines.

Here on our left commences Section G. the ground rising toward the south with considerable abruptness to the summit, thirty feet above the level of Indian Trail Avenue. Section N. is on our right. To save steps we notice a few of the lots and graves on the western slope of Section G. reserving the summit, eastern and southern slopes for a visit further on. Here are the lots of Judge Strong, Dr. Frederick F. Backus, John W. Tallman and Charles H. Chapin. The latter is enclosed with an iron fence. The pedestal of the monument supports a carved figure of ".. Hope," with upturned face and uplifted arm. Here rests Mr. Chapin. A head stone at the grave of his daughter, is similar to the one on the lot of W. F. Cogswell, more specifically described in another place. The next lots are those of E. O. Sage and C. F. Paine. The family burial place of Dr. E. M. Moore is here. On the opposite side of the Avenue, in Section M. are the fine monuments and lots of Deacon Oren Sage and Edwin Pancost. Just beyond and down the hill is where the late Judge E. Darwin Smith rests; a modest monument records the fact. On the left, in Section G. an evergreen hedge encloses the lot of the late Isaac Ashley. A few feet away is the lot, enclosed by an iron fence, where is buried the late Martin Briggs, and by his side reposes Hamlet D. Scrantom, an ex-Mayor of Rochester, and for years a commissioner of the Cemetery. Opposite is the lot of Hiram Blanchard, where is interred the lamented Hamilton H. Howard. The late John Haywood's is close by. In Sec. M. opposite the lot of Martin Briggs is the tomb of the late Dr. B. F. Gilkeson, whose memory is cherished by his professional brethren and by thousands to whom he had administered in the capacity of a physician. He was a noble man, and an enterprising, progressive citizen. Here is the grave of Joseph Curtis, who was a prominent citizen of Rochester. Closer to the Avenue rests Capt. Byron P. Thrasher, who laid down his life in one of the many battles of the rebellion.

Ex-Mayor Charles J. Hill rests in his lot on the east side of the Avenue. He was born in Woodbury, Conn., April 13th, 1796, and removed to the Genesee country in 1816, and became a citizen of Rochester. He commenced the milling business in 1831, and pursued it until 1876. He was president of the Pioneer Association and had held many offices of public trust, conferred by his fellow citizens. He was genial and sympathetic, quick to feel for the sorrow of others. His attachment to old friends and employees was remarkable, instanced in the late

Charles Buckley, who was in his service for forty years. He gave fame to the City of Rochester, and was vitally interested in its prosperity. He died July 19th, 1883, beyond the four score years. The world was better and happier for his having lived in it, and he sleeps remembered and honored by all and his deeds of charity and loving kindness do follow him.

A marble slab supported in a horizontal position by marble columns marks the tomb of James K. Livingston. Close by and on the same side, are the burial places of the late ex-Mayor Isaac Hills, Thomas Kempshall and Silas O. Smith. In this last lot rests ex-Mayor Edward M. Smith, who died in 1884, while acting as U. S. Consul at Manheim, Germany. The monument lately erected to the memory of Mr. Smith is one of the latest and prettiest styles of monumental work in the Cemetery. It is of Quincy granite, dark grayish color, of the recumbent cross style, resting on polished granite bases. The base is about 8 feet long, 4 feet wide, and 4 feet high. It has antique lettering. It came from the manufactory of H. S. Hebard.

In this immediate locality is the lot and grave of Everard Peck, who was one of the pioneers of Western New York and prominently identified with its history. A brief biography will not be inappropriate.

Everard Peck was born in Berlin, Conn., in
1791 ; came to Rochester in 1816, when the place
had less than 400 inhabitants. His original oc-
cupation of book-seller and book-binder led him
to the publication of a village newspaper, the
Rochester *Telegram*, 1818, and to the establishment of a large paper mill in connection there-
with. Retiring from that business a few years
later, he devoted himself during the rest of his
life to banking pursuits, being connected, suc-
cessively, with the Bank of Orleans, the
Rochester City Bank and the old Commercial
Bank. He was actively interested in many of
the charitable and educational institutions of
the City, being one of the founders of the
Orphan Asylum and largely instrumental in the
establishment of the University of Rochester.
He died on the 9th of February, 1854, respected
as one of the most useful and upright of our
citizens.

Observe from where we stand the lots of Dr.
James W. Smith, ex-Mayor Levi A. Ward and
of Wm. Brewster, who was for many years a
Commissioner of the Cemetery. Also the stately
monument on the lot of Louis Chapin. Cedar
Avenue, will take us along the southern border
of Sec. M. the western slope being occupied
with the single grave divisions.

It will repay the tourist to step over there for

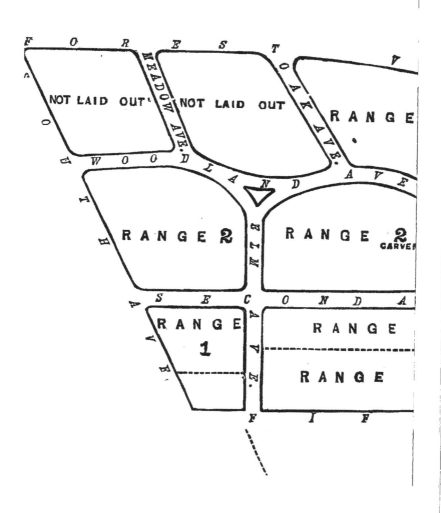

a few minutes. A board at the head of a grave, notifies in Chinese letters, that the body of Quan Hi rests there. His age, date of death, etc., is given. Quan Hi was a laundryman who conducted business on State street, Rochester, at the time of his death, 1876. The interment was under the management of Jeffreys, the undertaker, and the ceremonies were performed by Chinese, in accordance with their custom. Quan Hi was the only Chinaman ever buried here. In the fall of 1884, Chinamen in New York corresponded with Mr. Jeffreys in relation to the exhumation of the body and its shipment to China. A few weeks later, without assistance, the remains were disinterred by his countrymen, who came on from New York, and were subsequently sent to the Celestial Empire for re-interment.

By a narrow path we ascend the southern slope of the hill, Sec. G. to notice the lots of the late Frederick Whittlesey, Dr. Levi Ward, Wm. Burke, Judge Addison Gardiner, Judge Samuel L. Selden, George J. Whitney and John Allen, the latter an ex-Mayor of Rochester, who was known as the "poor man's friend," and whose memory is cherished by hundreds. The lot is graced by an elegant monument, erected by his sons, one of whom, Robert, has since been laid by his side. A beautiful sarcophagus has been

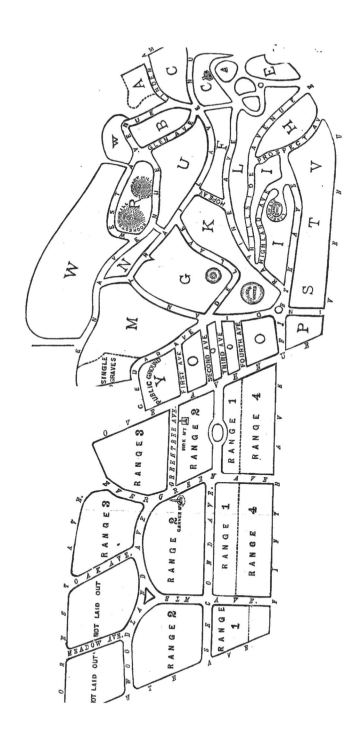

erected to the memory of Mr. Whitney. Samuel
D. Porter, that good man, is buried near here.
Close by is a fine lot with one of the finest monuments in Mount Hope. The shaft supports an
urn which is draped with the National flag. The
inscription reads " Lieut. Wm. Kidd, 2d U. S.
infantry, killed at Bull Run, August 30, 1862,
aged 19 years." Turning to the east we pass
Dell Avenue, notice the lots of Wm. H. Perkins,
who was killed in a railroad accident, Wm.
Mumford, Daniel Scoville, Wm. Pitkin, H. F.
Atkinson. Here lies the wife of the great
revivalist Charles G. Finney. A beautiful rustic
marble cross marks the peaceful abode of the
wife of Hobart F. Atkinson. A flight of granite
steps takes us to the lot of Edmond Lyon. A
massive granite coping encloses it with stone
walls, deep in the ground. It is catacombed and
arranged with stone sepulchers. The monument is a fine one, granite bases and a marble
shaft, supporting a nicely executed figure " The
Angel of Peace." A little to the right lies
Warham Whitney, and Gen. John Williams
sleeps his last sleep beside him. A little further
on are the lots of N. G. Hawley, James W.
Sawyer, George Hollister, and Joseph Putnam.
Here rests I. Henry Putnam of the Old 13th N.
Y. S. V. The next lot is that of Henry B.
O'Rielly. Lieut. Henry O'Rielly, who was killed

in battle, May 5th, 1862, while attached to the
Excelsior Brigade, is buried here.

On a circular mound close at hand is a plain
monument bearing the inscription, "Myron
Holley, born in Salisbury, Conn., April 29th,
1776. Died in Rochester, N. Y., March 4, 1841.
He trusted in God and loved his neighbor.
Dedicated in 1844. Erected by the Liberty party
of the United States of America, to the memory
of Myron Holley, the friend of the slave, and
the most effective as well as one of the earliest
founders of·that party." It is said that the cost
of the monument was defrayed by penny con-
tributions. A little further north are the lots of
Gen. L. B. Swan, Robert Hunter, ex-Mayor
Samuel G. Andrews, W. H. Cheney, James
Breck, J. B. Robertson, Jesse Congdon and
Luther Tucker. The lot of the late Aaron
Erickson is made strikingly attractive by a magnificent figure of "The Weary Pilgrim," recumbent upon a solid and appropriate base—the
work of Papotti, a great Italian sculptor.

In the same lot and east of the monument is
the burying place of Gilman H. Perkins. Pretty
tomb stones have been erected to the memory of
his dead children. A few feet north east is the
grave of Gen. E. G. Marshall, of "Old 13th"
fame. A monument in sarcophagus style attracts

the closest attention of the observer. A sheaf
of grain is nicely carved on the lid. The general was buried here August 5th, 1883.

The most elegant thing in the way of a head
stone in the cemetery, marks the grave of the late
Mrs. Wm. F. Cogswell. It is of pure white
American statuary marble, Gothic style, the
front panel having exquisitely carved upon it a
cross entwined with a Passion vine and flowers.
It was made at the establishment of H. S.
Hebard.

Notice here the lots of Jacob Howe, A. J.
Langworthy and Amon Bronson. The grave of
David K. Cartter, father of Judge Cartter, of
Washington, is on the northern slope of this
section. At a point nearly opposite of where
we are standing is a dell, or the old tunnel with
terraced banks. This is fifty feet deep and 150
feet in diameter at the top. We have finished
Sec. G.

Turning so as to face southwest, Second
Avenue runs a little to the right between Sec's.
O. and Y. The Potter's field is on the west side
of the section also on Sec. Y. while the single
grave localities are on Y. and the south border
of Sec. M. Cedar Ave. being the defining line
between the sections. We will go through
Second Avenue to Grove Avenue, the boundary
line between the old and the new grounds.

Standing on this elevation, the outlook over the new portion of the cemetery is grand. There are many who prefer the level, new grounds to the old, and have transferred the bodies of their friends thereto. Still the hills, ravines, dells, terraced slopes and stately trees of the old part are lingering in our memory and one cannot but love them. It has been the dwelling place of many of our kindred, and for us, when our mission is ended, to lie apart from them is not a pleasurable reflection. We will now proceed to the

FIREMEN'S MONUMENT.

Grove Avenue is the dividing line between the old and new grounds. A walk of five minutes westwardly takes you to the Firemen's Monument, situated on a high bluff overlooking the Genesee river, the City of Rochester, Lake Ontario and the surrounding country. It is a fitting resting place for the heroes who lie there awaiting the last command of the Chief Engineer of the Universe.

At its dedication, September 9th, 1880, there was an imposing display by the civic societies of the city. Andrew M. Semple, President of the Rochester Fire Department, was president of the day. Hon. James H. Kelly delivered the address and a historical sketch of the Fire

Department. The cost of the monument was about $8,000. On the east side of the monument there are twenty-seven little tombstones, and on the west sixteen, in honor of the individual firemen whose names they bear. The earliest date of death inscribed upon the marble is that of Thomas M. Rathbun, 1827.

The monument reflects great credit on the manufacturer, H. S. Hebard. It is of St. Johnsbury granite, and is without a flaw or blemish. It is of the Egyptian Doric style. We give its dimensions as follows : The platform is twenty-four feet and three inches square, two feet high, with square projecting corners, each surmounted with a beautiful granite vase. There are three half-circle steps on the front. From the platform an excellent view of the city can be obtained. At the foot of the bluff rolls the Genesee. The words "Fire Department" is the only inscription on the work. The first base is eight feet six inches square and one foot nine inches high. The second base is seven feet square by two feet ten inches high. The die is five feet square, five feet high, with beaded corners. The cap is six feet seven and a half inches square and five feet high, the lower portion having carved wings and globes representing Time and Eternity. The base for the shaft is four feet eight inches square and one foot nine inches high. The shaft is three feet six inches square and seventeen feet six inches high. On each face of the top of the shaft are engraved wreaths. The cap of the shaft is four feet six inches square by three feet four inches in heighth. The base for the figure is three feet ten inches square by two feet one inch in heighth. The figure is that of a fireman, wearing a fire hat, with coat on the left arm, in the attitude of rest on his return from a fire. The pose is excellent, and the figure is in every respect symmetrical. It is eight feet nine inches in heighth. The whole heighth of the monument is fifty feet. The lot or grounds have been nicely graded, with the intent to set out the monument and make it conspicuous.

THROUGH THE NEW GROUNDS.

In making the journey through the new grounds, we can save much time by commencing at the junction of Greentree and Grove Avenues, east of Forest Avenue, stopping meanwhile to notice the neat monument of Justin Riley. East of this is the lot and monument of Joel Eaton, and on the right, headstones mark the graves of the wives of George Potter and Robert Renfrew. We note also the lots and tombstones of

H. J. Weaver, C. C. Hayden, John Stack, Jacob Biesham, Joseph Hubecker, John Crede, John Turner, John Worms and John C. Shutte. On the north side of Evergreen Avenue, is the nicely kept lot of Charles Perkins. The inscription on a fine headstone states that his beloved daughter Emma, called away in the blossoming of life, sleeps here. Almost directly north of the Carver monument is the neat lot of George Weldon, and here rests his mother, two sisters and brothers, Henry and the lamented Walter Weldon. Near by is the lot of Eli Weed, with several fine head stones.

At the time the new grounds were laid out the Jewish citizens had broken away from the orthodox custom so long observed of burying their dead in congregational lots in the order of death. Meyer Greentree purchased a plat of ground on Evergreen Avenue 100 feet square, and, after reserving a spacious lot for himself, gave lots to others of his faith. In this same sub-division of Range 3, other Jewish associations, also individuals have lots, with reserved ground for the poor and strangers of their nationality. Lavish but judicious display is made by the wealthy lot-owners in beautifying their grounds, keeping them in order and erecting monuments and tombstones. The most striking is the Funkenstein monument, erected

by the widow of the late Levi Funkenstein, thus
showing her love and affection for her deceased
husband. On one face is the inscription "In
memory of my sister Deborah and infant, lost at
sea in the City of Glasgow, 1854." The north
face has the inscription Phineas N. and Sophia
Cardoza.

A nice monument notes the resting place of
Julius Bachmann. The pedestal has a marble
figure leaning upon an anchor. A world of
thought is conveyed in the words "Our good
brother" on the reverse side of the tombstone of
Joseph Buehler. A tasty and costly monument is
on the lot, and which marks the grave of Henry
Rosenberg. Then there are the lots of Lewis
Stern, Gerson Hochsteter, Moses Bronner,
Joseph Moerel, David Abeles, David Cauffman,
Ludwig Hechinger, Morris Savage, Louis W.
Moore, Henry Levi, Moses Blumenstiel, Samuel
Meyer. On the original Greentree lot are the
burial places of N. Rosenfield, D. E. Moseley,
M. Hart, Susan Holtz, H. Morofsky, Mark
Soloman, H. Lempert, S. Rubens, R. Jacobs, B.
Hermen, S. Rosenbaum, M. Goldwater, H.
Britenstool, M. Weinberg, L. Flesheimer, A.
Rosenthal, R. Schmitz, Mrs. Steefel, Mrs. Oppen-
heimer, F. R. Theis, A. Hydecker, L. Holtz, S.
Landau, M. Goldsmith, J. Rothchild, I. M.
Wile, I Wile, J. Wile, M. E. Sloman. In

another division are the lots of E. S. Ettenheimer,
Joseph and Gabriel Wile, Simon Hays, D.
Rosenberg, M. A. Savage, Elias Wollf, J. Cauffman, Moses Hays, M. L. Gutman, I. Rice, E. M.
Moerel, Lewis Stern, Samuel Stein, H.
Michaels and A. Adler. On the Stein lot two
little mounds cover the beloved remains of the
two little children of Wm. Miller. Elias Wollf
was the first person of his faith buried in Mount
Hope out of the orthodox custom, thus marking
an era of no little moment.

JAMES VICK.

Facing Greentree Avenue, on Range 2, lies
one who did more than any other man to en-
courage and cultivate the taste for flowers. His
was a household name all over this broad land
and in foreign countries. He reigned supreme
in the floral kingdom. Many, many years will
come and go before the name of James Vick is for-
gotten. It will always be held in grateful remem-
brance. He was supremely happy in making
others happy. He had no selfish thoughts or
actions. He lived not for himself but for all
mankind. In the church, sunday school, the
dwelling and work shop he cast sunshine all
around him. His memory will be ever green and

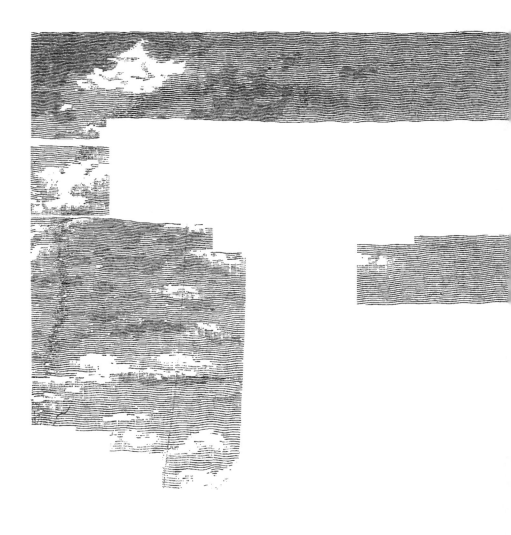

fondly cherished. His life on earth is the assurance that he dwells in the Floral Paradise above. He made the wilderness to blossom like the rose. What greater tribute can be paid to man?

> How sweet, how sweet are the lilies,
> And how we wait for their bloom
> We gather them in their glory
> And scatter them over his tomb.

A splendid granite obelisk monument, by many considered the nicest in its proportions, on the grounds, has been erected. A lily is cut on the west face of the obelisk.

On the next lot north is the grave of Capt. E. C. Williams. Passing along is seen the red Scotch marble monument of the lamented Dr. T. H. F. Hall, also the monument and tombstones of M. N. Van Zandt, D. Copeland, Wm. N. Emerson, John F. Selye, N. Tamblingson, Joseph F. Ely, W. D. Oviatt, M. Normington, Jacob Garson, L. C. Spencer and J. Gifford. The lot of Geo. Zimmer, at the corner of Grove and Second Avenues, is attractive, with a neat iron fence and marble monument. Nearly opposite the Greentree plat is the grave with a pretty headstone of Benjamin Brown, who was a railroad engineer, and who met with an accidental death. Nearer the Carver monument is the grave of Wm. H. Dawson, another railroad engineer who met an untimely death while on duty. The Dawson lot is one of the prettiest in the Cemetery.

Here we stand before the Carver monument, the highest (excepting the Firemen's) and most costly in Mount Hope. It was fashioned after the Trojan column at Rome, and manufactured by Peter Pitkin & Son, Rochester. The figure which surmounts the shaft was made by H. S. Hebard in the similitude of the one on the monument at Plymouth Rock. Dr. Carver was directly descended from the Carvers who came over in the Mayflower. The tablet on the west face has this inscription : " Dr. Carver was the father of the Pacific railroad. With him originated the thought of connecting the Atlantic and Pacific oceans by railroad." West are the lots of A. McLean, Gilbert G. McPherson and others.

On lot 177, but a few steps west of the Carver monument, sleeps one of the Nation's heroes, Lieut. Frederick G. Kislingbury, a victim of the Greeley Arctic expedition. Loving hands have placed his body here, and it is hoped that ere long sympathetic countrymen will erect a suitable monument to his memory. Woodland Avenue is south-west of this.

A little south and west of the Carver monument is the lot of Henry H. Craig, where sleep his beloved dead. It is neatly kept and beautifully located. Oak Avenue is next south of

Evergreen Avenue, and Meadow Avenue divides the new ground, which is not yet laid out into lots.

On either side of the Avenue are the burial lots of E. W. Tucker, Sigmund Stettheimer, H. N. Allen, Isaac Post, E. W. Pollay, Dr. Joseph A. Biegler, Samuel Rosenblatt, Jacob Mock, Samuel Busentheil, Jacob Blaesi, James Montgomery, Wm. H. Thomas, Hiram Smith, O. L. Angevine, W. H. Sheperd, John F. Stroh and C. H. and F. A. Rowe. Most of these have fine monuments. Near here is the lot of J. A. Hoekstra. The large granite monuments of Drs. Carpenter and Swinburne are elegant ones, and are quite conspicuous. The beloved physician, Dr. George Swinburne sleeps here, where his daughter, Mrs. Alice Newman, has erected the beautiful memorial. Between these monuments pretty tombstones mark where loving hands have placed the earthly remains of Kit Carson and Orra Maud, the beloved children of Hon. W. F. Cody, (Buffalo Bill). We turn into Elm Avenue and proceed to Second Avenue, between Ranges One and Two. On the right hand is the pretty monument of L. N. Millener. We pass the lots of Charles C. Brown, John A. Holmes, Lyman King and the large and fine monument of Austin Crittenden. Directly west of this point is the handsome lot of John C. Smith. Resting here is the late George B. Oberst, suddenly cut off in his youth.

Conspicuous here is the elegant monument of Morris S. Jackson, erected to the memory of William F. Rice and S. Coraline Jackson, who were killed in a railroad accident while on their wedding tour. Here are the lots of Joseph Beir, Frederick Wurtz, Thomas Kirley; and to the right is a cluster of nice monuments on the grounds of C. A. Kellogg, F. E. Day, J. O. Howard, Wm. R. Booth and Franklin Hinchey, Dr. L. R. Herrick, the renowned patent medicine man, D. A. Woodbury, N. Hayward, A. Rohr, Richard Dransfield, George W. and Charles T. Crouch, L. A. Pratt, Thos. Peart, P. M. Bromley, Capt. Dan. Bromley, Wm. Corning, Wm. Diehl. Wm. O'Neil, John Hulett, H. B. McGonegal, I. Tower, C. Widman, C. C. Starkweather, and S. G. Bush. These last are on Range 4. The Crouch monument is of Richmond granite, cottage style, with an urn. The McGonegal monument is 26 feet high, of Richmond granite, and both came from the works of H. S. Hebard.

We started on the new grounds, at the northwest corner of Range 3. We note the lots on this Range, in addition to those especially mentioned above, of A. W. Mudge, John Ferner, John A. Davis, John B. Simmerlink, Philip

Stape, Joseph Katz, E. Higgins, Wm. R. Mason, E. Morse, A. J. Reibling, John Mogridge, S. Lemon, Geo. R. Ryan, S. C. Van Hooser, J. E. Line, M. Hotchkiss, Geo. W. Crouch, Jr., Rochester Continental Lodge, E. Swanton, Jacob De Vos, M. Smeed, H. Lauterbach, J. B. Keeler, Ira M. Ludington, Hondorf, Aman, Horschler, Barnes, Tallinger and Ehwald, Shannon, Kneale, James Ratcliffe, Sellinger.

On Range 2, we find the lots of H. H. Edgerton, L. A. Pratt, J. Shatz, E. Ocumpaugh, Dr. Tegg, L. Lowenthal, D. D. Campbell, Sabey, Salter, John Baird, E. B. Beck, Stilwell, Henry Wray, Wm. H. Armitage, James Mathews, David McKay, F. C. Skillman, J. H. Pool, S. Y. Alling, Dr. W. M. Fleming, Joseph Everest, C. V. Jeffreys, W. H. Stearns, Leonard Ham, Jacob Schlyer, Thomas Dransfield, Rev. A. G. Hall, Edward Harris, N. S. Phelps, Geo. Bently, Wm. Oliver, F. Heilbronn, S. C. Donnelly, Wm. Zorn, Wm. H. Jones, H. C. Boughton, F. S. Stebbins.

On Range One, we also find the lots of Wm. Corning, Isaac De Mallie, John Dent, A. Sornberger, P. Neerner, Thos. Knowles, W. H. Yerkes, C. Gucker, G. Pauckner, Corbin, Kirby, Forcheler, Hooper, Schoenfield, U. Steinheiser.

On Range 4, in addition to the lots noticed above are those of S. G. Curtice, (granite coping around the grave), S. G. Wetmore, Rich, Kallusch, Shoecraft, G. Lauterbach, Diehl, Wm. Hamilton, (from whom the ground was purchased), Kipphut, W. J. McKelvey.

As we have gone over only one half of the territory to be visited, we must not tarry longer.

It is proposed to erect a Crematory on the river side, west of the Firemen's Monument.

We have returned to Grove Avenue and crossed through Sec. O. to Indian Trail Avenue, a little east of where we left it. In Sec. O. near the Scotch lot is the burial lot of Frederick Lauer; also the old lots of the Jewish congregations. One of them is now occasionally used for burials. An elevated lot on Sec. K. overlooking the tunnel before mentioned, the image of a deer being conspicuous, is that of Ezra Taylor. Indian Trail Avenue has its easterly terminus at East Avenue, which runs north and south, and is the eastern boundary avenue of the old grounds. Mt. Hope avenue is the public highway.

In Sec. S. at the junction of Indian Trail, Ravine and Fifth Avenues, is the handsome, circular and elevated lot of Hon. Freeman Clarke. A stone and iron railing encloses, and a fine and tall granite monument graces it. On the apex of the shaft is a finely cut cross, which is mirrored in Sylvan Waters.

SYLVAN WATERS,

The only thing of the kind in Mount Hope is very pretty. [See engraving]. Thousands of beautiful gold fish live in its waters, and the terraced banks invite the tired tourists to rest awhile, and while resting we can repeat the words :

" O World ! so few the years we live,
  Would that the life which thou dost give
      Were life indeed !
  Alas ! thy sorrows fall so fast,
  Our happiest hour is when at last
      The soul is freed."

If we take Fifth Avenue, the most direct route, on our way back to the entrance, we shall miss many fine sights on Ravine, Highland, Hillside and Prospect Avenues and Observatory Hill, the southern slope of which is directly before us. We will therefore take a ramble through Ravine, Hillside and Highland Avenues, in good time retracing our steps to take a final and fresh start. In the short jaunt spoken of, we take in portions of Sections L. K. and I. the southern parts of them. We note the lot of Rev. Charles E. Furman, a neat tomb stone marking where rests the beloved preacher. On the east side of Hillside Ave. is the grave of Edwin Scrantom (Old Citizen). The late Judge Geo. W. Rawson and Wm. S. Bishop, rest not far away. The family burying ground of the late W. Jerome Rogers is here, and to the right, up the slope, on Sec. L. a neat marble monument tells where reposes the wife of George Darling. On Sec. I. is the lot of Rev. James B. Shaw, and his precious dead there await the coming of the Lord. Eastward is the lot of Henry L. Fish. A granite pedestal supports two carved marble figures of a little child and a dog. Ex-Mayor John C. Nash is buried in a lot on Sec. F. while the lot of N. Osburn, which has a fine monument, is on Sec. L. A handsome lot made by filling up the ravine on Sec. K. on the left, is that of I. H. Dewey. It bears a fine Richmond granite monument, obelisk style, with a die and three bases. The shaft weighs about eleven tons. It is of a lightish gray color and came from the works of H. S. Hebard. S. W. D. Moore is buried near here. A neat marble monument marks the spot.

Further north and on Ravine Ave. are the lots of C. B. Woodworth, Edward Brewster and the late Lyman Churchill, Francis Gorton, Martin Breck, F. De Lano, Dr. H. W. Dean. The monuments are all fine ones. But we must return to Sylvan Waters. There is enough more in the localities we have just visited to occupy the attention of the tourist for several hours. East of Sylvan Waters and close by is the ele-

gant granite monument of Seth Green. The shaft supports a finely carved figure of " Hope," leaning on an anchor and with uplifted hand. Here the revered father and mother of Seth and Monroe A. Green sleep. Near it is the granite monument of H. D. Colvin, and a little further north rests George W. Parsons, with a headstone erected by the Sunday school scholars of the Central Church. Between Fifth and East Avenues is the fine granite obelisk of the late James E. Hayden. The marble monument on the lot of Charles J. Hayden is attractive. A granite slab in a horizontal position covers the tomb of the late Ezra M. Parsons. These are in Sec. S. as are also the lots of Henry S. Hebard, A. Vickery, Geo. P. Draper, David Hoyt and the late Rev. John Mandeville. We must tarry here a minute or two to notice the lot of John Quin, who spares no labor in its care. It is enclosed with an iron railing set in granite posts. The shaft of the monument was once one of the fluted limestone columns in the Main street porch of the old Eagle hotel building, the present site of Powers's building. It has a square cut stone cap and on that a stone cross. Several members of the family of Mr. Quin are buried here. Near here are the lots of Phillip J. Meyer and Jacob Schwendler, the latter having a sandstone monument.

Going back to Fifth Avenue, the ground on our left is on the eastern slope of Observatory Hill. On either side of the Avenue we notice the lots and monuments of Hiram Davis, J. Hubbell, L. Bauer, Rufus W. Main, Thos. S. Gifford, Wm. Y. Baker, Robert Turner, Timothy Wallace, Ex-Mayor Joseph Field, Ex-Judge Theron R. Strong and D. W. Fish.

Before going upon the summit of Observatory Hill, Sec. I. we will step a little to our right to see where lies Charles Backus, the once famous humorist and minstrel. Many a one to whose amusement and delight he catered in his and their lifetime, sleep near him. A fine granite monument has been erected to his memory by his wife.

The summit of Observatory Hill where we now stand was for years disgraced by a dilapidated wooden tower. It has been demolished, and it is hoped, ere many years have passed, will be replaced with a fine stone-observatory. The elevation is the most sightly in all Mount Hope. From it a birds-eye view of the surrounding country can be obtained. Broad fields, the vast nurseries, the pride of Rochester and the wonder of the world, farms yellow with golden grain, hills and valleys dotted with thriving villages, Lake Ontario, Irondequoit Bay, the Flower City, with its massive and costly

buildings, broad tree-lined avenues, the extensive public buildings of the County ; the glittering lines of steel with trains of cars speeding over them, form an enchanting picture. We are nearly two hundred feet above the level of the Erie canal aqueduct in the city. Below us and on our right is the distributing water works reservoir of the city. [See engraving]. From a magnificent fountain in the center of the reservoir, spring high into the air twenty-one jets of sparkling water. The central jet throws a column of water six inches in diameter. On the summit of the hill the lots of Wm. T. Simpson, Ebenezer Bowen, Gideon Cobb and Hiram Redfield are noticed. The neat lot of James H. Kelly is part way down the western slope, near Highland Avenue. It is hoped that the level hill top will not be further encroached upon with graves.

Again on Fifth and East Avenues, we visit the lots of Wm. Eastwood, Wm. Churchill, Asa Sprague, Joseph Hall, Charles and Homer Robinson, G. W. Leavenworth, Joseph Sibley, E. R. Hallowell, E. P. Willis, Isaac Rulifson and A. Babcock. These are on Sec's. T. and V. All of these lots have fine monuments. A little further north is the monument of the late H. S. Potter. It is a neat work. Two marble figures are on the pedestal, one in a standing position placing a crown on the head of the one kneeling. The

monument of Col. James Brackett and the late
A. J. Brackett is very pretty. It has a gothic
roof supported by polished Scotch granite pil-
lars. In the alcove thus formed is a carved
marble figure clasping a cross. We pass the
lots and admire the monuments of Mrs. E. F.
C. Emerson, Frederick Goodrich, Joseph C.
Stone, G. W. Burbank (a rustic marble cross) and
C. A. Jones. Near by was lately laid to rest
Joseph Stone, father of Newell A. Stone. He
had lived a decade beyond four score years, and
had seen Rochester grow from the wilderness to
a beautiful city.

Two large plats of ground in Sec. V. between
Fifth and East Avenues are enclosed by high
evergreen hedges, which prevent the beautiful
lots and works of art from being seen from the
outside.

Here are the family burying grounds of D.
W. Powers, Oscar Craig, Judge George F. Dan-
forth, Seth H. Terry, Lewis Selye, Dr. W. W.
Ely, Dr. Edward T. Ely, Elizabeth G. Elwood,
Wm. L. Halsey, George H. Mumford, Patrick
Barry, Ira Dunlap. The monuments here are
fine and much admired after access to the ground
is gained. The fine and costly monument of
George Ellwanger bears the carved marble
figure of St. John the Divine, the work of Papotti
of Rome, in a listening attitude and recording

the revelation from Heaven. "And I heard a voice
from Heaven saying unto me, Write, Blessed are
the dead which die in the Lord from henceforth :
Yea,. saith the Spirit, that they may rest from
their labors ; and their works do follow them."
Here rests Henry Brooks Ellwanger, the author
of many instructive works on roses. His life
was spent among the roses which he passionate-
ly loved. Surely his works do follow him and
his name will be honored wherever roses bloom.

We will here leave Sec. V. by descending a
flight of stone steps to Prospect Avenue, and
proceed to the foot of the hill lying between
Observatory Hill and the entrance, known as
Sec. H. Here is the tomb of Vincent Mathews.
L. L. D. An inscription on the monument states
that he was the father of the Bar of Western New
York. Higher up the slope are the fine granite
monuments of ex-Mayor Elijah F. Smith, Myron
Strong, A. M. Schemerhorn, Samuel Miller and
Martin Galusha. But we must not tarry but
return to East Avenue, and while walking to-
ward the entrance notice the lots and monu-
ments of D. R. Barton, A. F. and G. P. Wolcott,
P. B. Viele, John and Joseph Cowles, Mary L.
Cleminson, S. M. Spencer, George G. Cooper,
and J. Margrander. On Sec. L. on a lot enclosed by a hedge, Lieut. Geo. B. Force, 108th
Regt., killed at Antietam is buried.

Our tour is almost ended. A few minutes wil
suffice to pass over the lawns in front of the
Chapel and back of the entrance building. The
family vault of Peter Pitkin is on the right and
that of Dr. A. Pratt, nearly opposite on the left.
A tombstone notes the grave of the late John
Morton. The monuments on the lots of J. E.
Morey, Col John G. Klinck, G. W. Allen, F.
Nusslin, T. A. Newton, L. D. Patterson, D. A.
Woodbury, S. Sloan, and Dr. John B. Elwood,
are nice ones, the latter one of the finest in the
Cemetery. This lot is on the northern border
of Sec. L. Right here is the opportunity for a
person to make the choice between granite
and marble for a monument. On this plat is
the lot of the late Thomas Parsons, father of
Mayor C. R. Parsons. Noticeable here also are
the lots with pretty tombstones of B. Frank
Enos, Col. F. A. Schoeffel and the late Beverley
W. Jones. These places are on either side of
Elwood Avenue.

Just south of the Morey monument was
recently laid to rest, Dr. A. M. Bennett, who was
a highly respected physician of Rochester and
prominent in social circles, and near it is the lot
of A. Mosely. Two statuary marble headstones,
with sheafs of wheat finely engraved upon the
panels draws forth admiration. They are the
work of Trott & Weigand, monument makers,

Mount Hope Avenue. The late wife of John C. McQuatters sleeps in a fine lot on this plat, south side of Elwood Avenue.

RETROSPECTIVE.

The following places were not noted in the ramble : On the south-west part of Sec. Y. are the lots of the Episcopal Churches, Truant House, House of Refuge, Home of the Friendless, and Industrial School. The Odd Fellows' lot is on the north side of Sec. O. and the University lot is on the north-east corner of the same section. The Scotch Society lot is near the Odd Fellows' grounds.

In Sec. M. is the Masonic burial lot, old one, and the graves there indicate the faithfulness with which the principles of the Order in succoring the sick and caring for the dead are observed. At the time of the Chicago fire the society in Rochester had forwarded $1,500 to the sufferers when word was received that further aid was not needed. The balance of the money, $400 was voted to the purchase of a new lot in Range 2, on the new grounds.

The following were not noticed in the regular tour. — Sec. A. W. B. Morse. Sec. M. Grove S. Gilbert (Rochester's lamented artist),

C. Hanford, H. S. Fairchild, Harriet Lockhart,
Sec. R. Dr. M. M. Mathews. Sec. W. D. M.
Anthony. Sec. G. Gen. I. F. Quinby, E. H.
Hollister, H. W. Strong. Sec. K. S. G. Steele,
John Steele. Sec. L. F. Zimmer. Sec. H.
A. McWhorter, Chas. H. Yost. Sec. I. David
Dickey. Sec. V. C. T. Amsden, A. M. Hastings, S. D. Walbridge. Sec. O. Dr. M. Leyden, F. Tully. On the lot of the late Alvah
Strong, is buried the child of Dr. H. S. Miller.

We have gone over an immense amount
of ground, and have been economical of time
and exertion. Without the Guide it would have
been impossible to have accomplished and seen
so much. A person wishing to visit any particular locality and that alone will find the
shortest and easiest route in the Guide. The
sections are, geographically, puzzlingly lettered,
requiring specific directions to find their location. This difficulty is not encountered in the
numbering of the ranges on the new grounds.

STATISTICAL INFORMATION.

Previous to 1850 interments in Mount Hope
and, in fact, in all the cemeteries were under the
direction of a City Sexton, elected by the people.
Wm. G. Russell, David W. Allen and John H.

Thompson served in that capacity for many years. In 1850 James Hair was appointed Superintendent of Mount Hope, under the control of the Commissioners. He served until his death, 1864, with the exception of a few months, when his place was supplied by James G. Benton. Chauncey Parsons was his successor and acted as such for a year and a half, when George D. Stillson was appointed. He served from 1865 to 1881, when he was laid to rest. His son, George T. Stillson, the present Superintendent, succeeded him. It may be appropriately mentioned here that almost simultaneously with the advent of superintendents of the Cemetery, the Jeffreys undertaking establishment now located at 155 State street, Rochester, was inaugurated. Its first interment was in 1854, and since then it has officiated at the last rites of sepulcher for over ten thousand of our beloved dead, giving the utmost satisfaction. It has kept more than even progress with the vast and pleasing improvements that have been made in the conduct of funerals, the cerements of the dead and burial ceremonies. In fact it has initiated most of the new modes. Its name is familiar in nearly every household in Rochester and vicinity. It enjoys almost unlimited knowledge of the cemeteries of Rochester, and can give information concerning them hardly obtainable elsewhere. The improved, scientific method of embalming, first introduced here and pursued by this house, is far superior to the ancient custom of enwrapping the body in cloth saturated with preservatives and has done away with the unsightly ice box, while preserving the remains in perfect naturalness and life like appearance for an indefinite length of time. The growing custom of having private burials necessitates more than ever the services of such an experienced undertaking house.

At his appointment as Superintendent of Mount Hope Cemetery, Mr. George D. Stillson prevailed upon his life-long friend, Mr. Daniel E. Harris, to accept the position of Assistant Superintendent, which position the latter continued to occupy until his death, which occurred at Mount Hope January 14, 1875.

From the date of his first residence in Rochester, in 1814, Mr. Harris' family history was closely identified with that of Mount Hope. From infancy to manhood, and the closing years of his life, were spent upon, or in the near vicinity of the Cemetery grounds. He witnessed the many changes occurring in the gradual development of this wildest of Nature's retreats to its present perfect state of rural beauty ; and it was especially fitting that his earthly work should cease there, and his remains repose in the ground which has received so much care at his hands. In the exercise of his duties at Mount Hope Mr. Harris was brought into close relations with thousands of our citizens at times when their hearts were crushed with grief, and his gentle manner and ever tender sympathy won their respect, and bound them to him in a friendship that is still strong and bright. His grave is a short distance south of the entrance, in Section E.

A vast amount of confusion as to the ownership of lots in Mount Hope was occasioned by the loss of records in the care of John B. Robertson comptroller of the city in 1857. He had charge of the funds and records. A few of the latter were found in Canada, but even to this day the loss of the books is felt.

REMARKS.

The writer in his walks through the Cemetery found many quaint, queer, and, to him, amusing inscriptions on tombstones. Those who had them written, however, saw nothing in them but sentiments of reverence and love. It would be in questionable taste to reproduce them here. Those who are curious in such matters are

referred to publications on church yard litera-
ture.

Mount Hope is not the property of a private
corporation, but is owned by the City of Rochester. Within a few years iron pipes have been
laid through the grounds and pure water from
Hemlock Lake is supplied in frequent tanks for
the purpose of watering the graves and lawns.
The necessity for another public entrance grows
stronger every year. It would seem that the
establishment of a line of carriages to convey
visitors through or to any part of the grounds
would prove remunerative.

In preparing this volume the author had much
valuable assistance from Superintendent George
T. Stillson, who is a worthy successor of his
lamented father. His worth and ability is read-
ily testified to by the commissioners and lot
owners. To Assistant Superintendent Mandeville thanks are also given. Patrick Gaffney,
who has been foreman for many years, has a
retentive memory and is an ever present
encyclopedia of the Cemetery. He also has
thanks for assistance. Bowdish & Hoagland,
of the Arcade Photo, Co. have been kind in fur-
nishing views in the Cemetery for use in the
Guide.

A CHAPTER ON FLOWERS.

The old notion that floral memorial and funeral pieces must be composed entirely of white flowers, has happily given way to the conviction that all colors are suitable for the purpose. Some of the most beautiful pieces ever seen, have this season been issued from the conservatories of White Bros., Florists, corner of Main and Union Streets, and on the Thurston Road. They were artistically arranged in various colors, and gave utterance to the sentiment of those who ordered them. With years of experience, they stand in the front rank of Flower City florists and have aided in cultivating the tase for flowers at funerals, the decoration of lots and the adornment of graves.

> "In all places, then, and in all seasons,
>   Flowers expand their light and soul like wings,
> Teaching us by most persuasive reasons,
>   How akin they are to human things."

BEAUTIFUL FLORAL EMBLEMS.

On the next page will be found a photo engraving, after the Ives process, of a floral memorial emblem, made by the well known and experienced florists Newdahl & Holwede, 67 East Main Street, Rochester.

The reader will agree with us that it is extremely beautiful, not only in design, but in the arrangement of the flowers and leaves. Each flower speaks in its language, love and affection ; there is no symbolical misapplication, as is often the case where the memorial piece is made by unprofessional and inexperienced persons. Flowers are

" Emblems of our own great resurrection,
Emblems of the bright and better land."

It is a commendable custom that sanctions the covering of the bier and grave with flowery garlands, typical of our hopes, esteem and sorrow. It is also an ancient custom, and a beautiful one withal, to deck the tombs of our loved ones with cut flowers and plants. Newdahl & Holwede have great experience in that line, and attend to all orders promptly.

ELEGANT MONUMENTAL WORKS.

Mount Hope Cemetery contains a very large amount of artistic and elegant monumental work, obelisks, shafts, columns, head-stones, monolith and sarcophagus styles. Those of modern construction compare most advantageously with those of older make, especially in withstanding the effects of the weather. This arises from the fact that monument manufacturers, have, from

Ives Process.   Ramsdell, Rochester, N.Y.

experience been enabled to choose the right material, either in marble or granite. This experience is advisedly given their patrons by Trott & Weigand, Mount Hope Avenue, near the entrance to the Cemetery. Many specimens of their work can be observed in Mount Hope and other cemeteries, and in every case they are much admired. They do not make misapplications in engraving emblems upon memorial stones, and all their work is artistically executed, and at rates that are reasonable, and still suffice for the procurement of the best materials and bestowal of excellent work. Designs are furnished on application. The firm is composed of young men, who have made an enviable reputation in their line of business and they will strive to maintain it.

———————

On the lot of Samuel Miller, Sec. H. a granite stone has cut on the upper face the word "Samuel." On the inside is this inscription: "This child, aged 4 years and two months, died Oct. 3d, 1838, at 2.30 P. M., the precise hour that this Cemetery was dedicated; and his was the first body interred in it after its consecration."

INDEX.

ADDITIONAL INDEX.

The following were accidentally omitted from the regular index:

CPSIA information can be obtained
at www.ICGtesting.com
Printed in the USA
BVHW041430220219
540923BV00007B/329/P